DICK BOSS

Also by Stacy Conis and Brittany St. Wells

The Bitches' Guide to New York City

DICK BOSS

**HOW TO FIGHT BACK
WHEN YOUR BOSS IS A BULLY
BUT YOU WANT TO KEEP YOUR JOB
(WITH LATEST BULLYING RESEARCH)**

STACY CONIS AND *BRITTANY ST. WELLS*

ORANGE HILLS PUBLISHING
NEW YORK

Dick Boss: How to Fight Back When Your Boss Is a Bully But You Want to Keep Your Job (With Latest Bullying Research) is a registered trademark.

Copyright © 2018 by Orange Hills Publishing (Orange Hills Publishing LLC). All rights reserved.

Epub edition April 2018 ISBN 9781980774044 (eBook)

Library of Congress Cataloguing-in-Publication Data

ISBN 978-1-9807-74044 (Paperback)

Printed in the United States of America

18 19 20 21 22 BUT 10 9 8 7 6 5 4 3 2 1

Orange Hills Publishing, New York, New York

ORANGE HILLS PUBLISHING
NEW YORK

CONTENTS

To all those who suffer under bullies.
May you take action.—S.C. and B.S.

INTRODUCTION

THERE ARE DOZENS OF BOOKS and websites about dealing with workplace bullies. Many of them even provide steps for stopping bullying behavior. But despite the collective wisdom, the experts generally agree on one thing: *If you've got a bullying boss or co-worker, you're eventually going to need to quit your job.*

We don't agree.

In fact, there's hope for dealing with workplace bullying and this optimism comes from science. It turns out there are concrete steps you can take to stop a workplace bully — and the techniques often work.

This is a different kind of book about workplace bullying and its strategy is unique. We call our approach "verbal combat," but don't get the wrong idea. We don't think yelling and screaming are solutions to workplace problems. However, we do think confrontation has its merits. We'll tell you more about verbal combat in these pages. But first, a little about us.

My co-author, Brittany St. Wells, and I are unlikely authors. We aren't scientists, doctors, or academics. We're young women with college degrees. But, there's one thing we have in common with the aforementioned professionals: we love science. We love reading academic papers so much that this book has nearly thirty scholarly citations. If there's a book, journal article, or published paper about workplace bullying, chances are we've read it.

Brittany and I dug into the research on nonviolent aggression (the basis of bullying) in a hunt for answers. We scoured the science and data to uncover the reasons for bullying behavior. It turns out bullying has been studied as far back as the early 1800s. We read books and journals and took notes on what we learned. Then, we analyzed the data and came up with our own hypotheses on ways to combat workplace abuse. Next, we checked to see whether these practices had been used elsewhere with success. Finally, we drew up an anti-bullying action plan. The book in your hands is the result of our work.[1]

At this point, you're probably wondering why you should read the advice of a couple of college graduates over the wisdom of professionals. The reason is simple: We don't have important reputations to protect. We're not trying to generate speaking fees or sell you videos. We're not peddling consulting services to corporate America. This frees us up to tell it like it is.

For example, we're the only authors who will tell you that your employer won't help. If you're being bullied, your company Human Resources (H.R.) department isn't coming to rescue you.

Whatever you want to say about bullies, they get results. Yes, they infect teams like a virus and ruin lives. But, they contribute to the company bottom line. That's why approaching H.R. about a workplace bully is a bad idea. You may even become a target for *further* abuse if you speak up.

Our commitment to you is this: We're going to teach you how to combat workplace bullying on your own. *Alone.* Because that's the reality.

Finally, a serious note. If you're experiencing workplace threats or violence, put this book down immediately and contact law enforcement. If the welfare of anyone at your workplace (including you) is in danger, contact the authorities. These situations require immediate intervention and are beyond the scope of this book.

Dick Boss is a silly title for a serious book, but we wanted to draw attention to the problem of workplace abuse. Bullying takes a grave toll on the health and welfare of all employees and doesn't belong in the modern workplace. Now, let's try and get that bully off your back once and for all!

Yours,

Stacy Conis + Brittany St. Wells

CHAPTER ONE

IMAGINE IF THIS WAS HOW SOMEONE TALKED TO YOU:

"You're about as reliable as a used car. If only I could return you to the dealer."

"Come on! Pick up the pace! Are you sure you're a college graduate?"

"I have low expectations of you, and you meet them every time."

What would you say to someone who talked to you like this? If you heard these words from a friend or family member, you'd probably tell them off. (And they'd deserve it.) But what if your boss were the bully?

Thirty million Americans have been or are now being bullied at work.[2] If you're a victim of bullying, you're not alone. But what can you really do about workplace abuse and mistreatment? The facts are the facts: your boss has power over you. She can fire you. If you hunt for a new job, you'll probably need her as a reference somewhere down the line. And even if you don't use her as a reference, it's a small world. If your relationship sours, word may get around. Someday, someone may call her and ask for the word on you.

You deserve to go to work every day in a stress-free environment. You deserve to do your work in peace and in a place that treats you respectfully. You deserve to be talked to in a calm, professional manner. You don't deserve any kind of bullying: not by anyone, or at any time. Not even from your boss. You deserve respect.

Bullying is insidious. Once you experience it, it can change your outlook. It can cause you to lose your confidence in yourself and in your abilities at work.[3] You may even want to quit your job in a huff if you're subject to workplace bullying. But unless the bullying has morphed into abuse or harassment, we think the last thing you should do is let a bully push you out of a job. You deserve to stay at your employer if you like everything else about your job.

So, you may be stuck between a rock and a hard place. If you tell your boss to shove it, you'll be headed out the door with a box of your belongings in no time flat. But if you say nothing, the bully will keep walking all over you. We think there's another way to stop the bullying and keep your self-respect.

ABUSE DOESN'T GET A PASS

How do you know you're being bullied? Is there a difference between a boss having a bad day and a bullying boss? There is.

The difference is in the viciousness directed to the victim, and in the repetitive, ongoing, and intentional nature of the abuse.[4] Bullying is rarely a one-shot deal: no bully yells at you one day, never to repeat the behavior again.[5] Rather, bullying is a pattern that someone develops over time.[6]

In *Beating the Workplace Bully*, author Lynne Curry lists several potential warning signs that your boss is a bully. Does he cut you down, then brush it off with "just kidding?"[7] Are you afraid to talk to him, even about minor things, because no one knows what will set your bullying boss off?[8] Is everyone else in the department responsible for your boss's bad moods or failings? Everyone, that is, except your boss?[9] Does he refuse to answer questions pertinent to your job, leaving you in the lurch and affecting your

22

performance? Does he seem to delight in torturing you—calling you at six in the morning and forcing you to rush to work, only to arrive after nine himself?

If one or more of these rings true, you're dealing with a bullying boss.

We don't think you can change a bully. We don't think it's your job to bring them into the caring human race. It's unlikely you'll turn them into an active volunteer or someone who fosters kittens and gives everyone half-day Fridays. Bullies don't change, because what they're doing works for them.[10] Your goal isn't to change them, but to change how they treat you.

Maybe your bully will get smart and stop berating colleagues for mistakes he's made himself. Maybe he'll move onto a new target. While not ideal, that isn't your concern. Your concern is you. In this book, we're going to share real, practical advice to help you stand up to a bullying boss or co-worker, assert yourself, and continue to thrive at work.

After all, jumping ship to a new job isn't always an option. And unfortunately, bullies are everywhere. *The skills in this book will help you now and with future employers.* Even if you do find another job, you may very well find yourself at a new company with an all-new bullying boss.

Later on, we'll teach you how to screen future employers for bullying bosses during the interview stage—so you can avoid them before you even start. We think it's better to screen a new employer before you jump into the deep end.

YOU'RE NOT THE FIRST VICTIM

It's normal to feel singled out when you're the victim of a bullying boss or coworker. *"Why is this happening to me?"* You may say to yourself, *"What did I do to deserve this?"*

The reality is, a bully doesn't "have it out" for a specific person. Your workplace bully has bullied before and they'll bully again. *It's not personal.* Aggression is a tactic he's learned to use to deal with people he finds threatening.

Maybe the bully finds you threatening because you're good at what you do. Or maybe you're well-liked and friendly. He may feel threatened by your intelligence or maturity. Maybe he doesn't like the fact that you have a life outside of work or that you don't have time to socialize with the gang for after work drinks. Anything that makes you stand out from the crowd can make you a bully's target.

Once you leave your bully behind, he'll find someone else to target—and that's awful to think about. But remember: you can't change a bully, and you can't change your workplace culture. Your employer is responsibile for stopping workplace abuse.

Your job is to take care of yourself.

THE POWER OF ACTION

A study by Bennett Tepper, Professor of Management and Human Resources at The Ohio State University's Fisher College of Business, and Marie Mitchell, Associate Professor at the University of Georgia, found that the employees who stood up for themselves when faced with a bullying boss fared better psychologically than those who didn't respond at all.[11] Employees felt better about themselves because they didn't just sit back and take the abuse.[12] We'll talk more about the need to take action later. You can even draw on Dr. Phil McGraw's personal interaction advice: "We teach people how to treat us." No one will know your boundaries until you establish them. If you accept bad behavior, it may continue.

Leaving your job isn't always the best option. Even if you dislike your bullying boss, you may love your job: the projects you get to do every day, and the other people you work with. We're pretty sure you had to work hard to get your job, too. After all, we all know how hard it is to find a job that fits with your skills and interests—and pays you what you're worth.

SUMMARY

- There's a difference between a boss having a bad day and a boss who's a bully:

  - A boss having a bad day will usually recognize their bad behavior and apologize afterwards

  - A bullying boss will repeatedly take disrepectful actions over a sustained period of time[*]

- You can't change a bully's behavior, but you may be able to get them to stop bullying *you*. Don't try to change a bully's personality[†]

- Teach people how to treat you by changing how you react to bullying. (Think of the adage: "We teach people how to treat us.")

- Stand up for yourself in a calm, professional manner but never with anger or hostility

- Standing up against workplace abuse is good for your health[‡]

[*]Broome, Barbara A., "Dealing with Sharks and Bullies in the Workplace," *ABNF Journal*: (Winter 2008); 19, 1.
[†]Curry, Lynne, *Beating the Workplace Bully* (New York: American Management Association, 2016).
[‡]Smith, Sandy, "When Bosses are Bullies, Fight Back!" *EHS Today*, (2018).

CHAPTER TWO

THERE ARE DIFFERENT KINDS OF workplace bullies, all of whom exhibit subtly different personalities and behaviors. However, one thing remains constant across types: bullies are insecure.[13] If a bully was secure in herself and her role at the company, she wouldn't have to bully anyone. She'd leave other people alone. Confident people don't have to demonstrate superiority or dominance over others. Insecure people do.[14] The only exception to this rule is the sociopath, a specific type of antisocial personality. Sociopaths are often highly manipulative and controlling; they use gossip, lies and other tricks to get their way. They intentionally cause harm and feel no guilt, empathy, or remorse.

Just as there are many different types of bullies, there are a variety of workplace bullying behaviors.[15] Some bullies use overt or out-in-the-open aggression. This behavior can take the form of yelling or name-calling. Other bullies use covert or hidden aggression. They may sabotage an employee's work or spread untrue gossip. Bullying behavior is as varied as the bullies themselves.[16]

HOW THEY ATTACK

Some bully behaviors include:

• Unjustified criticism (nitpicking)

• Threats of firing

• Assigning tasks below the target's job description

• Overwhelming the target with too much work to ensure they'll fail

• Belittling or demeaning the target in front of others

• Spreading false rumors about the target (personally or professionally)

• Swearing/verbally insulting the target

• Ignoring the target (leaving them off of email conversations, excluding them from key meetings)

• Taking credit for the target's work

• Aligning others against the target

YOU CAN'T FIGURE OUT A BULLY

Why does your bully act the way she does? And what's behind her charming and rude behavior? Is there anything you can do to stay out of her line of fire?

"I try leave her alone on Mondays because she's usually moody and blows up about things. Her email makes her mad, too, so I never interrupt her when she's on her computer. If I do those things, I can usually avoid one of her blow-ups. Does she lash out at me without a reason? Sometimes. But, she's under a lot of pressure and has a lot of responsibilities. She's good to me and the team at work. She even pays for things like parties and birthday cakes for everyone. She's a good person."

The problem with trying to figure out a bully is that no matter what you learn, it doesn't help you improve your situation. You can make excuses for her, but it doesn't make things better for you at work. Walking on egg shells every day won't prevent her next attack. But changing your behavior will.

It's time to take action.

YOUR REACTION MATTERS

You can't predict or anticipate workplace bullying. The only thing you can control is how you react to it. The majority of employees cower in response to a bullying boss or co-worker. They're intimidated and uncomfortable, and they don't want to do anything to rock the boat.[17]

As we mentioned earlier, some bullies are up front with their bullying behavior. They'll mock, humiliate or yell at you when the whole team is assembled for a meeting. No one is likely to stand up for you either— because few people want to aggravate the bully. They know that if they speak up, they may be targeted next. If they're not the target of the bullying, they'll most likely keep their mouths shut.

Other bullies will operate behind your back by bad-mouthing you. They'll mock your work when you're not there to defend yourself. They may even make up lies and rumors about you, so that when you walk to your desk, people will turn and stare, thinking the worst of you. (And not of your boss.)

A bully may even fail to include you in department meetings, emails or events. They'll starve you for information so that you're short on details. They set you up to fail. Is it a true oversight, as they claim? Or is this more evidence of their bullying? You'll know the answer by how often this occurs. If it's a one-time thing, it may be an innocent mistake. If it's a pattern—it's bullying.

There's even bullying that's not out in the open, nor completely behind closed doors. It's that "Am I the crazy one?" bullying. Is your boss standing too close to you when he gives you feedback on your reports? Do you feel threatened or harassed? Does your boss stare at you or roll her eyes when you speak up at meetings? Maybe no one else seems to notice, but you've observed it again and again.

Whether it's out in the open or behind closed doors, bullying is bullying. And it's got to stop. Bullies have a lot of tricks up their sleeves, from the yelling and name-calling, to the bad-mouthing, belittling, and excluding. Sometimes, being bullied to your face almost feels better than being bullied behind your back—at least it's more honest. If you're bullied in public, your co-workers can vouch for the bad behavior they witness. If it happens behind closed doors, or in emails, you may feel like you're losing your mind. If you're left out of department meetings and off of email chains, that covert bullying can be even more frustrating and difficult to prove.

WHEN BULLYING IS A CRIME

For the most part, bullying itself is not a criminal act. How many bullies did you know at school who laughed at you, bumped into your tray in the lunchroom or told nasty rumors behind your back? We all knew those bullies. But we learned not to complain to teachers or the administration because there was nothing they could—or would—do.

It's the same at work. If your boss is yelling at you, calling you names, or muttering curse words under his breath, it's not a crime—unless it morphs into sexual harassment or discrimination. The difference between legal bullying and illegal sexual harassment and abuse often depends on the target's identity.[18]

If bullying is directed to someone of a protected (often minority) race, sexual orientation, age or ability, then it's firmly in the area of discrimination and is therefore legally actionable.[19] Some countries, including Australia, The U.K., Norway, Sweden and Germany, even have laws against workplace bullying.[20] But if you're the target of bullying and you're not a member of a protected group, in the United States, you have no legal leg to stand on.[21]

If you find yourself the target of sexual harassment or discrimination, it's time to start documenting. After each day's work, write down every bullying action— the date and time, what happened, and who witnessed it. You'll need all that documentation when you call an attorney.[22] If you signed an arbitration agreement when you were first hired, you might not have the opportunity to take your case to court. But whenever bullying becomes discrimination or sexual harassment, we encourage you to document it all. The information can be used in a civil suit, or to negotiate a higher severance package.[23] Because while bullying is something you can counteract by asserting yourself, sexual harassment and discrimination should never be tolerated. And these actions deserve the most serious response.

WHY ARE YOU BEING TARGETED?

But why is your boss bullying you? What's their objective? Some bosses are just malicious. Other bullying bosses have never learned how to manage and inspire their teams in a positive manner, so they use intimidation and undermining to cover up their own incompetence.[24] Stress is often a key factor for bullying bosses: pressure causes them to lash out more.[25]

Perhaps you're *too* good at your job and your insecure, bullying boss is having trouble managing you *because* you're a higher performer. Sometimes, employees who exceed expectations find themselves the victims of bullying because their boss doesn't want a stand-out employee—they want a yes-person. By doing a great job and outshining your boss, you might have made yourself a target for bullying.[26]

But if your boss is bullying you, he probably has an objective—most likely to force you out. How does bullying achieve the boss's goals? If a bully isolates you by failing to invite you to department meetings or team events, you'll lose your support system. Your colleagues will start to see you as an outsider, and they'll align with your boss.

It's much easier for the bully to eliminate you if you don't have allies at work.

Similarly, talking behind your back creates suspicion about you. Your co-workers might think *you're* the problem. Maybe *you* have it out for other people at work. If your boss is blatantly lying about you, making you the scapegoat, and your co-workers and even your boss's boss believes the lies–then you have a problem.[27]

Yet, still you may wonder, *why me*? Why am *I* the one? There might be a reason for the target on your back. Maybe you're too meek—and the boss knows she can get away with yelling at you because you won't stand up for yourself. On the other side of the coin, you might be getting too powerful. If you're outshining your boss without bringing him along for the ride, he might decide to take you down a peg (or several) to protect his own position in the company.

Maybe the bullying boss has figured out your weakness. He's noticed how defensive you become when you're criticized. Or how you can't handle yelling and rush off to the bathroom to cry in private. A bullying boss will use your weakness to their advantage.[28]

There are other ways your boss can make life hell for you without out-and-out firing you. Have you done the work and gotten praised for it, only to see it presented by the boss as *his* work, without giving you any credit? Or is your boss micromanaging you? Is she always looking over your shoulder and correcting how you do things, even when you get the desired result?

When Sheryl began her job at a nonprofit, she soon found she was overworked. Her new position combined two previously separate jobs: she was now the only assistant for both the Executive Director and the Finance Director. When Sheryl had told her boss that she was spread too thin, he asked her to account for her time in writing—breaking it down into five-minute increments! That just added to her problem. While it's not the same as being yelled at or harassed, micromanaging impedes your work and can thus be seen as bullying behavior.

You'll know you have a problem when the bullying becomes more "official." Has your office been moved without any notice? Has your job title changed, effectively demoting you? Have you gotten a poor performance review? Were you taken off a favorite account or project without warning?

These aren't subtle actions. They are hints that your bullying boss has it out for you!

In order to defeat your bullying boss, you have to have a game plan. Just like it's hard to talk to your crush in the heat of the moment, it's really difficult to respond to a bully in the minutes after she's berated you in front of an entire conference room full of your peers. You're hurt. You might feel embarrassed—and shell-shocked. You know you can't go ballistic on her, so what can you do?[29]

SUMMARY

- Bullying takes various forms, from out-in-the-open hostility and disrespect, to more covert, behind the scenes abuse that you rarely see

- Targets of bullying are selected for many reasons, which may include being friendly and self-confident. The research shows that both low-peformance and high-performance employees may be victims of workplace abuse

- Don't psychoanalyze a bully. Focus your energy on responding to the abuse by taking action

- Standing up for yourself in a professional way has benefical effects on your mental and physical health

CHAPTER THREE

WE GET IT. BEING BULLIED makes you feel powerless, especially if the person bullying you is your boss. You need your job. Maybe you also like your job. Even if you wouldn't mind a new job, sometimes getting one is not an option. It might have taken you months to find this job. Or maybe you've worked there so long, you're vested in their retirement plan. Or you're expecting a child—and children are expensive. Whatever the reason, it's your job, and if you want to stay, you have every right to.

But how's that going to work? If your boss is berating you, bad-mouthing your work habits, and talking about you to your colleagues behind your back, it's not time to turn the other cheek. It's time to make a plan.

THE FASTEST WAY

TO STOP BULLYING BEHAVIOR

Here's a little tip about bullies: what they hate most of all is being confronted. Bullies want you to be intimidated. They expect you to cower. That'll make them feel more powerful—and make them want to yell at you more, too. But what if you stood up to your bullying boss? What if you flipped the script? How would your bully react *then*?

SHOULD YOU POKE THE BEAR?

We know what you're thinking. What if I "poke the bear" by confronting my bully boss and then I'm fired?! We know you want to give your boss a piece of your mind after all he's done to you—but is that really the best idea?

When we suggest "confronting" your bully boss, we need to be clear: don't yell at your boss.

We know. Sometimes, your bully boss gets you so mad that you would feel totally justified in yelling back. And you want to yell—so much! Your bullying boss has pushed you to the edge of sanity by taunting you. Changing your work assignments without any notice. Moving your office down the hall, around the corner—to a room with no window. "Forgetting" to say hello when they see you in the halls. Acting like you don't work there when you still do. But remember, it's only in movies that an employee can flat-out yell at her boss without getting fired. While it may feel good in the moment, yelling or becoming

49

abusive yourself is *not* the answer. Instead, Tepper and Mitchell's form of "fighting back" is more of a passive resistance.

In Tepper and Mitchell's study, "fighting back" includes 1) ignoring your boss 2) playing dumb or 3) putting less effort to your job. Results of the study showed that employees who "fought back" or stood up for themselves in one of these passive-aggressive ways were less likely to feel like victims, and were thus better able to withstand the bullying and keep their jobs. Employees also felt better about their own job prospects and their employer if they stood up for themselves with these passive forms of resistance.

But we know you're wondering: were there any negative consequences? Didn't these "resisters" have their moment of triumph in the sun, only to face a severe reprimand, if not an out-and-out firing, soon after? Strangely enough, Tepper and Mitchell found that the answer was no. Their team of researchers went back to the same participants after the initial study to see if any bad career outcomes followed their passive bully-resistance. And they found that not one person noted a poor outcome.

Yet we do want to caution you about underperforming as a passive response, as this could hurt your team and perhaps your future job options down the line. Tepper and Mitchell's results don't mean that passive-aggressive resistance is the only way to respond to workplace bullying.

The main takeaway from Tepper and Mitchell's study is that targets of bullying feel better when they refuse to adopt a "victim mentality" and instead used passive forms of resistance to stand up for themselves. Therefore, resistance is definitely a great first step towards targets feeling more empowered—and more able to deal with the situation at hand. "Bullies learn quickly who will tolerate their antics and whom will shut them down."

Even in grade school, standing up for yourself and not letting the bully see you hurt is good advice. In Mechthild Schafer's *Scientific American* article, "Stopping the Bullies," middle school principal Cindy

Seddon tells schoolchildren dealing with bullies to stand up for themselves, and to refrain from showing hurt or emotion: "By not showing weakness, a child can lessen the chance that a bully will target him or her." The rules don't change in the workplace. If you stand your ground with a bullying boss, she'll be less likely to provoke you again because she'll see that bullying you doesn't work.

Of course, not every bully is worth responding to. Is the bully a client who rarely visits the office and most often sends nasty missives via email? Then it's probably not worth your time or effort to respond. But if the bully is your boss, who you have to interact with every day, then you need to decide if it's worth standing up for yourself. What would happen if you didn't react? Would the bullying stop? Or would it most likely continue?

The choice is yours. You can refuse to react—if it's someone not worth your time or if you simply prefer not to engage in confrontation. But then, you must be prepared for the consequences. With no response, the bullying will most likely continue until your performance suffers, your health declines, and you feel forced out.

If that's not what you want, you need to stand up for yourself—as soon as possible, and immediately after the next incident! By standing up for yourself right after being bullied, you've set your boundaries and marked yourself as a tough nut, instead of someone who is easy to intimidate. Your bravery will lead the bully to find weaker prey elsewhere. Even if you're unable to stop the bullying boss, psychologically, you'll feel better for having stood up for yourself.

There is something very empowering about drawing your own boundaries and making it clear that you're not someone to be bossed around. You have your limits and you're going to demand professionalism, no matter what your boss or your company thinks is acceptable. Of course, if you find yourself in a company that encourages or enables bullying, then all your efforts to stand up for yourself may not end the bullying. In that case, you may need to admit that

you're in a toxic workplace that can't be cured. No
matter what type of workplace you find yourself in,
you have the option to stand up for yourself. Draw the
line. Make it clear what you will tolerate and what
you won't.

A BULLYING RESPONSE PLAN

Confronting your boss isn't for everyone. Maybe
you're a shy person. When faced with bullying,
maybe standing up and walking away is more your
style. Or maybe you'd prefer to ignore your bullying
boss. But if you decide to confront him, here are some
comebacks that allow you to be the good guy while
making it clear that your boundaries remain firm.

1) Anticipate the Attacks

You'll need to respond instead of react. This has to be
part of a thought-out plan.[30] In the moment, you'll

probably want to scream bloody murder. But that's not going to get your bully off your back. Take the time to think about how you're going to respond *before* you're actually in the heat of the moment. Will you ignore your bullying boss? Pretend not to notice their outburst? Walk away? Or have a comeback? You might need to think of a few different options and practice different scenarios at home with friends.

2) Keep Your Cool

Losing your cool is a trap we want you to avoid, as it's a sure way get yourself fired.[31] But we understand the dilemma. If you let your boss bully you without responding time and time again, your emotions and frustration get bottled up. Then, when you finally do respond, without a thought-out plan, you might very well explode. That's what happened to one Executive Assistant, Nicole, who let her boss, Stan, ignore her, exclude her from department activities and bully her for months on end. Then, when Stan had taken Nicole into a conference room to confront her about her attitude, Nicole wasn't prepared. She let her emotions get the best of her. Nicole exploded, yelling at Stan and letting him know how ineffectual and abusive he was.

Was Nicole telling the truth about Stan's management capabilities? Yes. Was her emotional reaction a quick way to unemployment-town? Unfortunately, yes.

Letting your emotions rule your response to a bullying boss means you're not in control. And despite her boss's bad behavior, once Nicole had reacted emotionally, she lost her ability to get the upper hand. H.R. heard about the confrontation and quickly made plans to give Nicole an exit strategy from the company.

That's why we recommend you to step back, assess the situation from the comfort of your own home and develop a well-thought-out comeback.

3) Have a Comeback

Stand up for yourself by talking back to the bully. Not in the unhinged, bombastic manner that they took with you—but rather in a calm, "I have my s**t together" manner that's going to throw the bully completely off-guard. You need to have a plan of action.[32] We'll share some specific comeback possibilities later on.

If your bullying boss yells at you and smears your work performance in front of other people, take a moment, and then calmly say something to them.

No bully likes being called out on their bad behavior. Setting your limits in front of not only your boss but also your co-workers lets everyone know you have limits.

You're putting your boss on notice. This way, your bullying boss knows that if he tries that again, you're going to stand up for yourself and cut him off—every time. Also, while few bosses would enjoy being told to calm down by an employee, asking your boss to speak with you professionally is understandable and will not land you in the flaming hot cauldron you'd find if you lost your cool and yelled back.

The trick to responding calmly and professionally is planning your response ahead of time. You need to be prepared so you can respond in the moment, instead of seething and building up resentment. When dealing with a bullying boss, you can't let an insult or a smear go by unremarked. That makes you as an easy target. We want you to be prepared with some comebacks or strategies so that you can respond in the moment and cut the bully off immediately, letting them know that this abuse can't happen again. So ask a friend to practice with you outside of work. They can be the boss and hurl an insult your way.

4) Walk Away

If you don't want to step out and say something to your bullying boss directly, remove yourself from the situation. Next time your boss loses it and starts to berate you, take a breath, collect yourself, say that you need to take a minute and then leave the room. You can make it a brief trip to the bathroom or a quick walk outside: whatever it takes to calm yourself down so that you can respond appropriately. Remember—if you get emotional, raise your own voice to match the bully's, or respond with snark, then the bully has won. Your response will only escalate her aggression.

5) Play Dumb

Ignore your bullying boss. What a bullying boss wants more than anything is a reaction. They want to know they've rattled your cage. You're on edge.

You're unsettled. If that's obvious to your boss, the bully has won. Just like a fish in shark-filled waters, you don't want to panic. It takes practice, but if you're able to keep your cool and act like nothing happened, your bullying boss will be the one on edge. Then, he'll go looking for his next victim in other waters. As Lynn Curry says in "Beating the Workplace Bully:" "The best defense against the humiliator: never let it show."[33]

COMEBACKS YOU CAN USE

Here are some comebacks you can use when you're faced with a bully:

"Wow, that sounded really harsh. Do you want to rephrase that?"

"I'm going to need you repeat that. But this time, make it respectful."

"Please don't talk to me like that. I'm not a five-year-old."

"I don't respond to yelling. I'm happy to talk with you when you've calmed down."

"We can sit down and discuss this when you're ready to speak to me professionally."

"We're coworkers. I don't respond to bullying."

"I don't deserve to be treated that way. Please try speaking to me again, but this time give me the courtesy I deserve."

HUMAN RESOURCES: FRIEND OR FOE?

H.R. likes to tout itself as the department to go to for help when you're having difficulty with a colleague, a work issue, or your boss. But here's the little dirty secret that H.R. doesn't want you to know—

H.R. doesn't work for you. They work for the company. That means H.R.'s priority is the company. *Not* you. Those who go complaining to H.R. may soon find themselves the targets of not only bullying, but also official problems like poor performance reviews and being labeled a "complainer."

In a recent study of H.R. responses to claims of bullying, H.R. was the *least* supportive of targets when they brought the claims against their bosses themselves.[34] In these cases, bullying bosses had 76% of management and 56.3% of their peers supporting their behavior. By contrast, only 3% of H.R. representatives supported the targets in cases of bullying. Targets of bullying found their support network elsewhere: their sympathetic co-workers, outside friends, and their spouses or partners. Remember, H.R.'s loyalty is to management—not to you.

If your boss is a bully and hasn't been fired yet, that's because they have support in the company. Most bullying bosses have enablers or co-conspirators who enable them to keep bullying—whether by joining in, or simply by staying silent.

Allowing a bully to flourish in a workplace is a clear sign of a lack of leadership. You may find yourself in an "a-hole friendly" organization. This means that competition is encouraged and high performers are rewarded, no matter how they conduct themselves. If that's the situation you're in, we don't recommend going to the very office that's supporting the dysfunction.

Remember, "If you let them, they will do it." You don't want to be the innocent bystander who says nothing in the face of abuse. Furthermore, studies have shown that employees who stand up to their bullying bosses feel more empowered and therefore fare better in the face of their bullies than the workers who shy away and don't respond. As psychologist and family therapist Dr. Jeff Gardere said, "The benefit for the victim is letting it out and letting it go."[35] Or as Dr. Gail Saltz, a Clinical Associate Professor of Psychiatry at New York Presbyterian Hospital said, "Rather than pretending, transparency, and authenticity have a way of making you feel better."[36]

Bullies don't expect you to react. That enables them to keep bullying. If you're willing to stand up for yourself, the bully will learn you can't be pushed around, and you'll find your footing at your job is a lot more secure.

TELL, OR
DON'T TELL?

Bullying can make you feel isolated because no one knows the stress you're under every day. The lies. The nitpicking. The texts to your phone when you're out to lunch or doing an errand. You're under so much pressure, and you want tell someone. But whom? Can you tell a coworker what's going on?

Most of your coworkers have a "survivor's instinct" at the office. That means they're unlikely to take your side for fear of antagonizing the bully. It's not that they don't care about you. They don't want to be victimized either!

Remember, alliances at work change all the time. Someone you call a "friend" at work one week may become your bullying boss's favorite the next. So, you have to be careful whom you talk to because it may get back to your boss. In fact, your boss may already be hard at work trying to isolate you from your work friends. (A common bullying tactic.)

Instead of sharing your troubles *at* work, we suggest you look outside of work. Find someone supportive and reach out to them if you need a shoulder to lean on. Whatever you do, keep the topic of bullying out of your work conversations. Don't divulge too much, because you never know who's on your side.

Having a support system is essential. Talk with your friends, family, or a significant other to air your feelings. That way, you can unburden yourself without the information traveling back to your office.

HOW TO SURVIVE

WHEN YOU'RE UNDER ATTACK

Now that we've affirmed all your suspicions about workplace bullying, you know those eye rolls you see from your supervisor aren't all in your mind. Those emails he just "forgot" to include you on were not accidental. And when your workspace was moved to a remote corner of the office—far, far from your peers—well, that sign was pretty obvious.

But what are you going to do? How are you going to maintain your sanity while you're standing up for yourself and confronting your bullying boss? We understand—it's not easy to maintain both your composure *and* your mental health when you're under assault day after day. That's why we've put together some tips to keep your mind clear and your body relaxed while under the gauntlet of a bullying boss.

When your daily reality is like a battlefield, just getting to the end of the day without screaming or crying can be quite an accomplishment. And as we mentioned before, your boss is bullying you with the hope of unnerving you. She wants you to lose your cool. She wants to hear you explode and yell so loudly that the whole office hears the commotion. Because that's when the bullying boss has the upper hand—when you lose your cool. And that's when they can easily get rid of you.

But we're not going to let them get to you.

Bullying can definitely take its toll. In one study, 23.5% of respondents "were bothered by frequent or constant thinking about the bullying."[37] The way to survive and keep your sanity intact while dealing day-in and day-out with a bullying boss is to keep their bullying out of your head. Don't let them take up residence in your most important part of yourself— your brain. As renowned bullying experts and founders of the Workplace Bullying Institute, Gary and Ruth Namie, recommend: don't be an accomplice in your own bullying by blaming yourself or thinking about yourself in a negative light.[38]

Because once the bullying seeps in and you start to believe all the horrible things your bully is saying—that's when you've lost the battle, and it's time to put down your sword.

Instead, remember that the bully's bad behavior is about them—it isn't about you. Retrain your mind so you paint yourself in a positive light, and don't take the blame for the bully's bad behavior. If you can't do this on your own, it's time for a therapist to help you on your journey back to wellness.

Some other great survival strategies for making the most lemonade out of those lemons include:

- **Exercise** – sweat your stress out!
- **Humor** – use it to put your bully off guard
- **Meditation** – helpful for staying centered
- **Deep Breathing** – great for keeping your cool
- **Journaling** – don't focus on the negative, or it'll make it worse

In such a combative and toxic workplace, you need a distraction—so you don't become obsessed with the bully at work. Remember, while you can't control the actions of your bullying boss, you *can* control your response. If you feel victimized and don't act, you'll become more depressed and less pro-active, and you'll sink into a funk that will be hard to escape. However, if you confront your bullying boss with the techniques we described in "Should you Poke the Bear," or decide that you need to plan your exit, you'll regain control and lessen the strain of having to deal with a bullying boss day-in and day-out.

SUMMARY

- Assert yourself! Stand up in the face of bullying because it will buoy your self-esteem and let the bullying boss know she can't push you around

- Be prepared! Never respond with emotion

- Have comebacks ready. You can practice them with a friend

- Use humor to deflect bullying behavior

- Play dumb—pretend you don't know why the boss is blowing their top

- Walk away. Remove yourself from the situation until the boss has calmed down or you can respond rationally

CHAPTER FOUR

W E ALL KNOW THAT FEELING. When you can't get out of bed in the morning. You're not fatigued, but sick at the thought of going into work. You have a headache almost every day. And all your friends have headaches after listening to your complaints about work and your bullying boss for the umpteenth time. Sometimes, there's nothing you can do but head for greener pastures. Sometimes, the bully cannot be tamed or dissuaded.

Sometimes, you just need a new job.

SHOULD YOU LEAVE YOUR JOB?

Staying at your job despite your bullying boss is only beneficial if it's the right choice for *you*. No matter how much your bullying boss makes you want to explode—we implore you—don't stay just to prove your bullying boss wrong. You might "win" and make your point: that your boss is a bully and is acting unprofessionally. But if the job and the company are not a fit for you, your win will be short lived. Stay in the job only if it's in your best interests.

We know—we've spent this whole time telling you it's going to be OK. You can stand up to your bullying boss and keep that job you worked so hard for. Except sometimes, there's nothing you can do. Sometimes, a situation is so bad, so traumatic, that you have to leave it—even if the future is uncertain. Even if you don't get the plum corner office or the posh parking space near the elevators. Sometimes, your mental health is more important.

BEFORE CALLING IT QUITS

1. Has your physical and/or mental health suffered because of your bullying boss?

2. Has the bullying escalated to abuse or harassment?

3. Are you no longer able to enjoy family, friends or activities because you're so stressed?

If any of these are true, then you need to make an exit plan.

The good news is that once you decide to make an exit plan, you'll feel more in control. You'll have options. And you'll know your bullying boss is not a permanent fixture in your life. Much like standing up to your bullying boss, making a choice—the choice to go—will empower you. And you'll realize you're not a victim. Your strength lies within you.

Sometimes, an office culture is so corrupt, so damaged, that the only sane thing you can do is get out. You might be in an "a-hole friendly" organization—a highly competitive atmosphere where cooperation and collegiality is not important. The only thing valued is who gets the "prize." Who wins the account, or makes the most money or racks up the most sales. If you're in a sink-or-swim atmosphere that embraces bullies, then it's time to get out. In addition, if your bullying boss has the confidence of *their* boss and/or the CEO, then you're not going to win, no matter what you do.

STRESSED ALL ALL THE TIME?

When your friends, family, and loved ones have heard your complaints about your bully and are showing signs of wear, it may be time to consider professional help.

Taking care of yourself should be your priority. You can't excel as an employee or in your personal relationships if you're stressed all time. And you shouldn't have to spend your waking hours outside the office worried about going to work, or replaying your bully's latest machinations.

Your bullying boss may hurt you, but that doesn't mean she has to succeed in bringing you down. You're the healthy one, and you can work to make decisions that are in your best interest.

If you find that your relationship with your boss is unhealthy and isn't showing signs of improvement, it's time to take the next step. Reach out to a counselor or therapist and get the professional help you deserve.

A SUPER SECRET JOB HUNT

ON THE SLY

You need a new job—but you're still at your current job. How's that going to work out? Luckily, we know some spy-skills to help you conduct your super-secret job search, while temporarily sticking it out with your bullying boss for the paycheck.

Number one – As tempting as it is, don't use your work computer to look for jobs You may feel secure. You may think that no one's paying attention to you. But someone is always paying attention. I.T. and execs sometimes get feedback on where their employees browse the Internet. You don't want them to see you on Netflix or a porn site, and you don't want them you to see you on Indeed.com either.

The solution? Bring your laptop to work. If you have an office, you can search for jobs on your laptop, having it open right beside your regular monitor. But this is a ballsy move, because someone may walk in at any time. So, only try this if you have a modicum of privacy, quick keyboard fingers and your back facing a wall so that no one can see over your shoulder. If this is too ballsy for you, use your laptop at lunch. No one can question you for that.

Number two – Get ill! Soon, you'll be going on lots of interviews, and of course you know enough not to say you're going on interviews. You have an illness. Preferably one a doctor can write a note for. Even if it's just allergies, your doctor can write a note that you need allergy shots (or something of that nature), and you can present the note to H.R. to get you off the hook. Then, when you tell your boss you have some upcoming doctor's appointments, legally, they can't ask you what the appointments are about. If they don't know their legalese and ask you anyway, just say "Everything's fine. I just have some recurring doctor's appointments I need to take care of."

Number three – Make your lunches count. Several times a week, catch up with someone for an informational interview about your job search. Ask them to keep it on the sly, because you're just starting to explore. Of course, the more informational interviews you have, the more word will get around that you're looking, and hopefully, the more interviews you'll get. Lucky for you, anyone with a job is always more appealing and more hirable than anyone without a job. So bullying boss or not, use that employed status of yours to your advantage. Do your research, be prepared, and choose the best fit for your next step.

SUMMARY

- When your health suffers, it's time to start looking for a new place to work

- When bullying becomes harassment or overt abuse, it's time to go!

- Once you make the decision to leave your job, you'll feel more in control. Dealing with your bully in the short-term will be easier

- If your bully situation isn't improving, use your time as a "gainfully employed" person to conduct a super-secret job search

- It's OK to be excited about a new job, but remember that bullies exist in every office. You just don't want to work for one!

CHAPTER FIVE

IF YOU'RE BEING VICTIMIZED BY a workplace bully, you have every right to want a quick fix. You're in the midst of a mountain of pain and you need relief— fast.

That's why it's common for people in the same situation to hunt for a new job in the hopes it will solve their bully problem. After all, what are the chances they'll get *another* bullying boss or co- worker? If they could just get out of their job and go somewhere else, it'll be smooth sailing, they think: nothing but sunshine and blue skies.

Unfortunately, the reality is a little different.

Maybe the next bully they encounter won't be their manager or co-worker. Maybe it'll be a client, someone in I.T. or the head of a department they have to work with.

The reality is that bullies will appear throughout your career, and that's because there are bullies at every company. Plus, bullying is part of human nature.

Being hopeful about the future is important. And it's right to want to end a bad work experience immediately. But if you do jump ship, use the skills below to screen your prospective boss and employer. Ask questions beforehand so you don't get stuck with another bully. Learn as much as you can before you go start somewhere new. That's the best way to avoid another bully or a hostile work environment.

IMPROVE YOUR BULLY RADAR

Start by understanding where bullies thrive. Bullies flourish in industries where high-ranking employees work with low-ranking employees. They're also common in high-pressure and high-stress environments. If you've worked in medicine, law, finance, advertising, media, broadcasting, or entertainment, you've probably seen your share of bullies. These industries attract type-A personalities who can be both aggressive and demanding.

Some people who are currently employed in these fields may feel like they have to tough it out in a bad environment to prove their mettle. It's a badge of honor to survive a brutal environment, right? A medical professional screams at you during the workday—so what? A creative director curses you out—it happens. An entertainment executive throws a tantrum and bashes your desk—grit your teeth. It's just part of the job, people say. But is this your goal?

Do you want to endure mistreatment just so that you can rise in the ranks of a toxic workplace?

THE LATEST BULLYING RESEARCH

In 2017, Gary Namie, co-founder of the Workplace Bullying Institute, updated his periodic survey of workplace bullying. He'd completed it in 2014, 2010, and 2007 as well. The results? Namie found that bullying was still prevalent in American businesses.[39] As you might suspect, although both genders bully, more men are bullies, and more women find themselves the targets of bullying. 70% of perpetrators of abusive, bullying conduct are men, with 66% of all targeted workers being women. According to Namie's study, only 30% of bullies were female.[40]

Sadly, workplace bullying remains an issue because so few targets address or even acknowledge that it's happening. Namie's survey showed that "29% of targets remain silent about the abusive conduct; only 17% seek formal resolution."[41] With so few targets speaking or standing up for themselves, bullies feel free to abuse their workers with impunity. Until there are consequences, either from the target, the organization or preferably both, bullying will most likely remain a workplace reality, lowering productivity and confidence for both those bullied and those who witness it.

According to Namie, even when organizations learned of bullying, they were often ineffectual if not downright harmful to the bullies' targets. In 46% of reported bullying cases, employers investigated the complaint inadequately and targets reported that nothing changed. Only 23% of the targets said their employer's investigation resulted in positive change. And a mere 6% of bullies were harmed by the reporting.

Most targets still opt to evade bullying by leaving their job. In 54% of bullying cases, bullying only stopped when the target lost their job, either by choice or being fired. The one bright spot in Namie's study is that 77% of his participants agreed more laws need to be put in place in the United States to combat workplace bullying.[42]

This exodus of hard working, well-trained workers due to their bullying bosses' abuse will only stop when targets learn to stand up for themselves, and when bullying is treated with the same severity in the United States as it is in other countries, including the U.K., Norway, Sweden and Germany. Only then will targets be protected and will bullies finally get their due.

MAKE SURE YOUR NEXT BOSS

ISN'T A BULLY

If you do have to leave your job because of a bully, we hope you found the tips in the Super Secret Job Hunt section helpful. During your job hunt, we hope you get lots of interviews, too. This will give you a chance to practice screening your next potential boss to make sure he's not a bully.

The problem with interviews, of course, is that everyone is on their best behavior—especially bad bosses. So, how do you know whether the boss you're interviewing with will have the same personality once you're hired? What follows are some questions to ask during an interview.

There are a couple of things to keep in mind. Don't let the answer to one question sway your opinion about the employer or the company too heavily. The answers you receive should be reviewed in total to get a full picture of the prospective boss and the company. Also, tread lightly. These questions are sensitive. You don't want to ask them rapid-fire during a first interview: you should use them at a second or third interview. Think of the process as a dance: you want to ask these probing questions when you're sure they're interested in you. Otherwise, you may come off as caustic or unpleasant.

Here are some questions to use to get insights into a boss and the culture at a company:

1) How long was the person who previously held this role in their position?

The answer to this question may give you insight into the employer's workplace culture. If the previous employee had a short tenure in their job, it could mean the company has a hostile work environment, or it could mean the employee didn't get along with their boss. It could also mean nothing. As with all answers you receive in an interview, be on the look out for lack of candor. Lies are common in job interviews, so it's likely you won't get honest answers to all your questions. Ask your questions anyway.

2) May I ask why this person left the company?

The answer to this question will provide key insights to the work culture at the place you're interviewing. The best reason you could hear is that they got promoted internally. Any hesitation by the interviewer in replying to your question might be an indication that things didn't end well. That could mean there were problems with the boss or the previous employee.

3) How involved is top management in day-to-day operations?

Get a sense if there's harmony or dissension between workers and management.

4) How does your team handle stress when things get hectic?

Assume that all workplaces have crunch times. But you want to see how the boss manages them and how she expects her team to perform.

5) How do you prefer giving your employees feedback? What types of informal and formal reviews are in place to let employees know how they're doing?

Be on the lookout for open and honest feedback. Any potential boss who's averse to giving feedback or thinks you should just "figure it out" may be someone to avoid.

6) Can you talk about how your department works together as a team?

See if the boss talks positively about teamwork or seems more competitive and cut-throat.

FIND A GREAT WORK ENVIRONMENT

After months or even years of workplace bullying, when you finally have an interview, we get it. You're excited. This is going to be the greener pasture you've been dreaming about. Everyone is going to be nice and respectful. Cooperative and engaging. Nary a bully in sight. But before you get your hopes up, we have a few words of caution. After all you've been through, we'd hate to see you wind up in an all-new situation with an all-too-familiar problem: another hostile workplace. So after you steam press that suit, buff up those shoes and get your hair cut to look A+ for your interview, don't forget to do your due diligence to make sure you avoid another hostile workplace.

On the lookout for a hostile workplace? Before, during, and after the interview:

- Talk to your friends
- Get the vibe
- Do your research
- Ask to meet the team you'll be working on

Just like everyone has an opinion on anyone they've ever met, we all have opinions about places we've worked. Once you have an interview lined up, tell your friends. Does a friend of a friend work there? If so, take them out to coffee. Ask them some key questions like "What do you like about this company?" "Do you feel encouraged and supported?" "Do you have any gripes or cautions you'd like to share?" Get the sense if they are excited about going in to work every day—or wary. If you are able, chat with a few people so that you don't get one person's potentially skewed view.

The vibe of the company will be apparent as soon as you come in. Is the receptionist friendly or aloof? Does anyone offer you water, or do they ignore you? Are people rushing around with purpose, or do you see a lot of web surfing? Often, when a company has a toxic vibe, you can feel it in the air. Something just seems awry. All the assistants are hot, young women and all the execs are men. Or the boss comes over and snipes at the receptionist right in front of you. Take notice of the general tone of the office and add that first impression to your list of things to consider before taking a new job.

Of course, we all know we should research a company before we interview to work there. But you can also research their reputation. Glassdoor.com lists anonymous employee reviews, so you can see if there's a general joy about working there, or a common thread within the complaints. Be wary, however, of the lone complainer who gives a company one star while everyone else gives four or five. At any workplace, there's always going to be someone who's unhappy. What you're looking for is a consensus on the company you might join. If one person says they're miserable, but everyone else feels respected and professionally supported, you're probably in a good place. But if 80% of the reviews are negative and they all mention the CEO being short-sighted, or note the rampant nepotism in promotions—then you'll know what you're getting yourself in for.

And finally, don't just meet the boss during your interview. If you're lucky enough to get a second interview, ask to meet some of the team you'd be working with. Seeing how they interact will give you a good sense of whether it's a supportive team or another toxic environment you'd rather avoid.

CREATING A BETTER LIFE

The best part about working for a bully is learning how to screen potential bosses so that you'll never have to work for a bully again.

When we first start our careers, no matter what field we're pursuing, we're often pretty wide-eyed and optimistic. Yet, after suffering through months or years of working for a bullying boss, it's like we've gone through our very own bullying boss boot camp. Never again will you take a boss's put-downs personally, or let a snide comment slip by, or consider your boss "like a family member" or a "friend," now that you know the truth. Your boss, whether they're a bully or wonderful person, is your supervisor. And they're flawed, just like everyone. Of course, having a flawed boss is par for the course. It's having a bullying boss that you'll never put up with again.

Once you've worked for an actual bully and suffered that emotional abuse for far too long, you'll know your boundaries. You'll know how to sniff out a bullying boss at the interview stage, or figure it out when your current boss leaves and a new bully comes to replace him. But this time, a bullying boss won't catch you off guard. And she won't affect your perceptions about yourself.

You now have the tools to keep your cool and stand up for yourself by responding appropriately, but firmly. It won't seem strange to you to stand up for yourself by saying, "I'm sorry, I don't find that appropriate." Or to stand up in the middle of a review and state "You're yelling, and unfortunately, I find that unacceptable. We can reschedule for when you're calmer." Once you've had a really terrible bullying boss, it's amazing how clear everything becomes — what's worth putting up with and what isn't. How you deserve to be treated and what you expect from your workplace. Because while many people love to say "my office feels just like family," we know that's not true, not even in the best of circumstances. Work is not family. If you mess up, family can't fire you. They don't give you official reviews. And they don't control how much you get paid.

But after working for a bullying boss, you're not looking for family, or for utopia. Instead, you're looking for what you deserve: a supportive, healthy workplace with guidelines in place to stop bullies in their tracks. We can't promise that you'll never have another stressful situation at work. Or even that you won't have another bullying boss. Unfortunately, there's just too many of them to avoid the whole lot. But we hope we've given you the tools and the insight to stay five steps ahead. So the next time you encounter a bullying boss, you'll know how to reduce their power, protect your personal boundaries and keep their toxic behavior from invading your head. We wish you much success as you continue to thrive in your chosen career, while standing up to any bullies that may come your way.

SUMMARY

- Bullies come in both genders, but more men are bullies than are women

- Bullies target women more often than men

- Research a future employer carefully to ensure you know the vibe and can avoid bully-culture

- Ask any potential new supervisor targeted questions to weed out the likelihood that you'll be a victim of workplace abuse

- Once you've had a bullying boss, it's like "bully boot camp"—because you'll be aware of the tricks bullies use. You'll never be duped again!

ACKNOWLEDGMENTS

A book like this wouldn't be possible without the scholars who are at the forefront of workplace bullying research. We owe our gratitude to the following: Gary Namie, Ruth Namie, Lynne Curry, Dana Wilkie, Robert Mueller, Sandy Smith, Margaret Kohut, Barbara A. Broome, L. Arseneault, Lila C. Carden, Jill Schachner Chanen, Angela Stelmakowich, Gina Vega, Michelle Cleary, Arthur H. Bell, Ronald M. Shapiro, Patrick McCormick, Noa Davenport, Sam Horn, Bennett T. Tepper, Walter

Frick, Anna Almendrala, Margorine A. Cassell, Mechthild Schafer, Jodran Timm, Keli Goff, and Adrian Furnham.

A special thanks to our agent, Vanessa Kundler, who's been our rock during the past twenty-three months. Our deepest thanks to the staff at Orange Hills Publishing, including Marson and Robert. And, a big hug to Faroosh Abda for her scrupulous editing of the many manuscripts we FedEx'd from across the country.—*S.C.* and *B.S.*

REFERENCES

Almendrala, Anna. "The Case For Sticking Up For Yourself At Work." *Huffington Post* (Jan. 22, 2015).

Arseneault, L., L. Bowes, and S. Shakoor. "Bullying Victimization in Youths and Mental Health Problems: 'Much Ado About Nothing'? *Psychological Medicine* 40 (2010).

Bell, Arthur H. *You Can't Talk to Me that Way!: Stopping Toxic Language in the Workplace*. Franklin Lakes, NJ: Career Press, 2005.

Broome, Barbara A. "Dealing with Sharks and Bullies in the Workplace." *ABNF Journal* 19, no. 1 (Winter 2008).

Carden, Lila C., and Raphael O. Boyd. "Workplace Bullying: An Ethical Context Applying Duty and Outcome based approaches to Human Resource Functions." *Southern Journal of Business & Ethics* (2010).

Cassell, Margorine A. "Bullying in Academe: Prevalent, Significant, And Incessant." *Contemporary Issues in Education Research* 4, no. 5 (May 2011).

Michelle, Cleary, Garry Walter, and Michael Robertson. "Dealing with Bullying in the Workplace: Toward Zero Tolerance." *Journal of Psychosocial Nursing* 47, no. 12 (2009).

Curry, Lynne. *Beating the Workplace Bully*. New York: American Management Association, 2016.

Davenport, Noa, Ruth Distler Schwartz, and Gail Pursell Elliot. *MOBBING: Emotional Abuse in the American Workplace*. Ashland, Ohio: Civil Society Publishing, 1999.

Frick, Walter. "What Research Shows About Talking Back to a Jerk Boss." *Harvard Business Review* (April 9, 2015).

Furnham, Adrian, *Backstabbers and Bullies: How to Cope with the Dark Side of People at Work*. London: Bloomsbury, 2015.

Goff, Keli. "Should You Confront Your Old Bully?," *The Daily Beast* (Aug. 4, 2014).

Horn, Sam. *Take the Bully By the Horns*. New York: St. Martin's Griffin, 2002.

Kohut, Margaret R., *The Complete Guide to Understanding, Controlling and Stopping Bullies and Bullying at Work*. Florida: Atlantic Publishing Group, 2008.

McCormick, Patrick, "Pick on Someone your Own Size," *U.S. Catholic* 70, no. 5 (Sept. 2005).

Mueller, Robert. "Bullying Bosses: A Survivor's Guide: How to Transcend the Illusion of the Interpersonal," www.BullyingBosses.com, 2005.

Namie, Gary. "2017 Workplace Bullying Institute U.S. Workplace Bullying Survey," Workplace Bullying Institute.

Namie, Gary and Ruth Namie. *BullyProof Yourself At Work*. Benicia, CA: Double Doc Press, 1999.

Schachner Chanen, Jill. "Taking a Bully by the Horns." *ABA Journal* 85, no. 8 (August 1999).

Schafer, Mechthild. "Stopping the Bullies." *Scientific American* 16, no. 2 (2005).

Shapiro, Ronald M. *Bullies, Tyrants, and Impossible People: How to Beat Them Without Joining Them*. New York: Random House, 2005.

Smith, Sandy, "When Bosses are Bullies, Fight Back!" *EHS Today* (2018).

Stelmakowich, Angela. "The Fear Mongers." *OH & S Canada* 21, no. 7 (Oct/Nov. 2005).

Tepper, Bennett T., Marie S. Mitchell, Dana L. Haggard, Ho Kwong Kwan and Hee-Man Park. "On the Exchange of Hostility with Supervisors: An Examination of Self-Enhancing and Self-Defeating Perspectives." *Personnel Psychology* (2015).

Timm, Jordan. "Are You an Office Tyrant?" *Canadian Business* 84, Iss. 11/12, (July 18, 2011).

Vega, Gina and Debra R. Comer. "Sticks and Stones May Break Your Bones, but Words Can Break Your Spirit: Bullying in the Workplace." *Journal of Business Ethics* 58, no. 1/3 (May 2005).

Wilkie, Dana. "Where the Bullies Are." *HR Magazine* 61, Issue 2 (March 2016).

ENDNOTES

1. The publisher, its employees, and assigns assume no liability for the use, misuse, results, or consequences of the information in this book, now or in the future.

2. Gary Namie, "2017 Workplace Bullying Institute U.S. Workplace Bullying Survey," Workplace Bullying Institute, 3.

3. Dana Wilkie, "Where the Bullies Are," HR Magazine 61, Issue 2 (March 2016): 56.

4. Barbara A. Broome, "Dealing with Sharks and Bullies in the Workplace," ABNF Journal 19, no. 1 (Winter 2008): 28-30.

5. L. Arseneault, L. Bowes, and S. Shakoor, "Bullying Victimization in Youths and Mental Health Problems: 'Much Ado About Nothing'? Psychological Medicine 40 (2010): 717–729.

6. Lila C. Carden and Raphael O. Boyd, "Workplace Bullying: An Ethical Context Applying Duty and Outcome based approaches to Human Resource Functions," Southern Journal of Business & Ethics (2010).

7. Lynne Curry, Beating the Workplace Bully (New York: American Management Association, 2016), 14.

8. Ibid.

9. Ibid.

10. Ibid.

11. Bennett T. Tepper, Marie S. Mitchell, et al., "On the Exchange of Hostility with Supervisors: An Examination of Self-Enhancing and Self-Defeating Perspectives, Personnel Psychology 68 (2015): 723–758.

12. Sandy Smith, "When Bosses are Bullies, Fight Back!" EHS Today (2018).

13. Margaret R. Kohut, The Complete Guide to Understanding, Controlling and Stopping Bullies and Bullying at Work (Florida, Atlantic Publishing Group, 2008), 218.

14. Wilkie, "Where the Bullies Are," HR Magazine, 56.

15. Angela Stelmakowich, "The Fear Mongers," OH & S Canada 21, no. 7 (Oct/Nov. 2005): 36–42.

16. Gina Vega and Debra R. Comer, "Sticks and Stones May Break Your Bones, but Words Can Break Your Spirit: Bullying in the Workplace," Journal of Business Ethics 58, no. 1/3, (May 2005): 104.

17. Keli Goff, "Should You Confront Your Old Bully?," The Daily Beast (Aug. 4, 2014).

18. Patrick McCormick, "Pick on Someone your Own Size," U.S. Catholic 70, no. 9 (Sept. 2005): 44.

19. Noa Davenport, Ruth Distler Schwartz, and Gail Pursell Elliot, MOBBING: Emotional Abuse in the American Workplace (Ashland, Ohio, Civil Society Publishing, 1999), 174–180.

20. McCormick "Pick on Someone your Own Size," 44.

21. Ibid.

22. Robert Mueller, Bullying Bosses: A Survivor's Guide: How to Transcend the Illusion of the Interpersonal (San Francisco, BullyingBosses.com, 2005), 256–258.

23. Davenport, Schwartz, and Elliot, MOBBING, 174–180.

24. Wilkie, "Where the Bullies Are," HR Magazine, 56.

25. Ibid.

26. Stelmakowich, "The Fear Mongers," 37.

27. Mueller, Bullying Bosses, 19–22.

28. Curry, Beating the Workplace Bully, 16–17.

29. Arthur H. Bell, You Can't Talk to Me that Way!: Stopping Toxic Language in the Workplace (Franklin Lakes, NJ, Career Press, 2005), 86.

30. Ronald M. Shapiro, Bullies, Tyrants, and Impossible People: How to Beat Them Without Joining Them (New York: Random House, 2005), 13–19.

31. Ibid.

32. Curry, Beating the Workplace Bully, 53–5.

33. Ibid.

34. Tepper, Mitchell, et al, "On the Exchange of Hostility with Supervisors," 723–758.

35. Goff, "Should You Confront Your Old Bully?"

36. Ibid.

37. Walter Frick, "What Research Shows About Talking Back to a Jerk Boss," Harvard Business Review (April 9, 2015).

38. Gary Namie and Ruth Namie, BullyProof Yourself At Work (Benicia, California: Double Doc Press, 1999), 242–244.

39. Ibid.

40. Ibid.

41. Ibid.

42. Ibid.

Made in the USA
Middletown, DE
07 February 2021